Keyboard Percussion

CHRISTMAS FAVORITES

Solos and Band Arrangements
Correlated with Essential Elements Band Method

ARRANGED BY
MICHAEL SWEENEY

Welcome to Essential Elements Christmas Favorites! There are two versions of each holiday selection in this versatile book:
1. The SOLO version (with lyrics) appears on the left-hand page.
2. The FULL BAND arrangement appears on the right-hand page.

Use the optional accompaniment tape when playing solos for friends and family. Your director may also use the accompaniment tape in band rehearsals and concerts.

Solo Pg.	Band Arr. Pg.	Title	Correlated with Essential Elements
2	3	Jingle Bells	Book 1, page 7
4	5	Up On The Housetop	Book 1, page 7
6	7	The Hanukkah Song	Book 1, page 19
8	9	A Holly Jolly Christmas	Book 1, page 21
10	11	We Wish You A Merry Christmas	Book 1, page 21
12	13	Frosty The Snow Man	Book 1, page 25
14	15	Rockin' Around The Christmas Tree	Book 1, page 25
16	17	Jingle-Bell Rock	Book 2, page 8
18	19	Rudolph The Red-Nosed Reindeer	Book 2, page 8
20	21	Let It Snow! Let It Snow! Let It Snow!	Book 2, page 8
22	23	The Christmas Song	Book 2, page 29

ISBN 978-0-7935-1767-1

7777 W. BLUEMOUND RD. P.O. BOX 13819 MILWAUKEE, WI 53213

Copyright © 1992 HAL LEONARD PUBLISHING CORPORATION
International Copyright Secured   All Rights Reserved

JINGLE BELLS

Bells Solo

Words and Music by J. PIERPONT
Arranged by MICHAEL SWEENEY

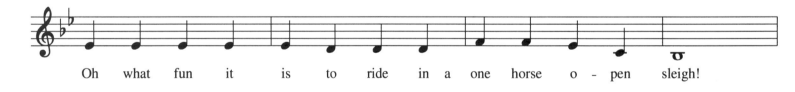

UP ON THE HOUSETOP

BELLS
Band Arrangement

Arranged by MICHAEL SWEENEY

Moderately Fast

Bells
Play

00862516

Copyright © 1992 HAL LEONARD PUBLISHING CORPORATION
International Copyright Secured   All Rights Reserved

THE HANUKKAH SONG

Arranged by MICHAEL SWEENEY

THE HANUKKAH SONG

XYLOPHONE
Band Arrangement

Arranged by MICHAEL SWEENEY

FROSTY THE SNOW MAN

Words and Music by STEVE NELSON and JACK ROLLINS
Arranged by MICHAEL SWEENEY

Bells Solo

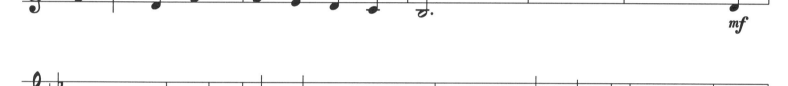

ROCKIN' AROUND THE CHRISTMAS TREE

BELLS
Band Arrangement

Music and Lyrics by JOHNNY MARKS
Arranged by MICHAEL SWEENEY

Rudolph the Red-Nosed Reindeer

Music and Lyrics by JOHNNY MARKS
Arranged by MICHAEL SWEENEY

BELLS
Band Arrangement

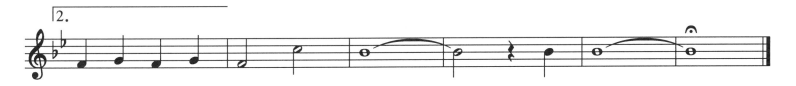

00862516

Copyright © 1949, Renewed 1977 St. Nicholas Music, Inc., 1619 Broadway, New York, New York 10019
This arrangement Copyright © 1992 by St. Nicholas Music, Inc.
All Rights Reserved

THE CHRISTMAS SONG

Music and Lyric by MEL TORME and ROBERT WELLS
Arranged by MICHAEL SWEENEY

BELLS
Band Arrangement